Walking Out of the Shadow of Death

MY MIRACULOUS JOURNEY FROM COVID WIDOW TO BRIDE OF CHRIST

REBECCA KRAEMER

Text copyright © 2022 Rebecca Kraemer
Walking Out of the Shadow of Death

Published by Radical Reformation Revival

All rights reserved.

No part of this publication may be reproduced, distributed, or transmitted in any form or by any means, including photocopying, recording, or other electronic or mechanical methods, without the prior written permission of the publisher, except in the case of brief quotations embodied in reviews and certain other noncommercial uses permitted by copyright law.

The moral right of the author and illustrator has been asserted.

Cover design by 100 Covers
Book Production & Publishing by Miramare Ponte Press, LLC

Hardback ISBN-13:978-1-959213-05-5
Paperback ISBN-13:978-1-959213-06-2
eBook ISBN-13:978-1-959213-07-9

Introduction

This is an odd little book. It's about my present. It's about my future.

But it's also about *your* present and your future.

I tried to be transparent. It's a book that I never intended to write, so apply mercy in abundance when I fall short.

I share my surprise as well. The revelations are personal to me but the principles are powerful for us all.

As I walk out of the shadow of death and darkness, I can see the LARGENESS of our God. I am walking out changed.

With His help, I tell you about my ongoing journey, trusting that you will find some encouragement, strength, and even direction.

ONE
This Is Me

I met my husband of 50 years on a blind date my first weekend at college. Although I was not impressed, I agreed to another date. (Good way to meet other guys!) I was from out of town and knew no one. To my surprise, this man grew on me. He was kind, a gentleman, had lots of friends, and was a good kisser (very important in those days). All those things made me overlook the fact that he loved cowboy boots, hockey, and liked to party. We married three years later.

We came to Jesus together during a major health crisis of mine. I was near death and had come home from the hospital with a private duty nurse named Sandy. That was 45 years ago, but I remember her as quiet and compliant. I sensed something "different" about her and insisted that she tell me what it was. She stammered, unsure how to respond to my very direct tone. I can still remember her words, "Well, I guess it could be that I'm a Christian."

I quickly shouted, "I want it! How do I get it?"

Meekly she replied, "I guess we could pray." We stumbled through a very short prayer. Since she was only two weeks old in the Lord, our prayer was anything but polished.

I was changed by the time I put the period on that little novice prayer. I was ruined for the ordinary and radically passionate about my Jesus—with very little wisdom. My poor little nurse was put in the middle of a spiritual tornado.

My Richard came home that night to a changed woman. He was amazed but skeptical. Sandy's Christian friends came over and Jesus moved into his heart as well. Our world had forever changed. Our journey with Jesus had begun—our somewhat bumpy journey. As people would say, it's our "You should write a book" journey.

TWO
This Was Us

Rich and I loved God together for all those 45 years. We're certainly not well known for great spiritual works. We're not renowned leaders. We had many God adventures together, many disappointments, and we loved God together.

At four years old, we sold our home and quit our jobs to join a wonderful ministry, Youth With A Mission (YWAM). That was 10 years of coming face to face with the Father Heart of God, the Power of the Blood of Jesus, and our very human humanness as well. That time forever changed us.

We were ordained through Christian International. We had opportunities to learn to lead big groups and little groups, take outreaches to many countries, and even have a church in our home for 12 years. We've mentored, prayed for the sick, and done deliverance.

Rich and I prayed together every day. We prayed for our nation, its leaders, and the raising up of leaders in every area of influence in our culture. We daily prayed Psalm 91 aloud together every day, declaring our protection. We prayed for our children, grandchildren, and every Christian family worldwide. We called back to God the prodigals of every family. We prayed for the Church, God's Ecclesia, to rise and make a stand. We prayed for the raising up and releasing of every generation, from the very young to the very old. We prayed for the "greater things will you do" stuff for when the Church will walk in the authority to carry that power. We prayed for Bridal revival and a Home Church movement to accommodate the fast growth of harvest. We prayed for the protection of the prophets.

We've had hardship and troubles. The Bible says we will. There's been business bankruptcy entwined with betrayal, a house fire and losing everything, major health issues, and family challenges. Like you, I'm sure, the list is long.

But I can say with absolute certainty, God's Word is true.

 And we know that in all things God works for the good of those who love him, who have been called according to his purpose.

— ROMANS 8:28

I know that Rich would agree.

THREE

The Shadow Rolls In

One morning, Rich woke up focused on getting ready for work as usual. In passing, he remarked that he must be getting his yearly cold because he had a little cough and runny nose. But off to work he went.

The next morning, his symptoms had increased but he wasn't concerned, after all, that's how his colds were. He grabbed a big box of Kleenex and again went to work.

The next morning, he had significant "cold" symptoms. I convinced him to stay home from work and hydrate himself. We had an IV nurse come to our home and give him an IV of water and vitamins. He felt somewhat better and slept all day.

I, however, started to have similar symptoms. That caused me to call our primary care provider to see if we could come in and have her listen to our lungs. Maybe we needed some antibiotics? Due to the Covid pandemic, the doctor wouldn't let us come inside the clinic but listened to our lungs in the parking lot while we sat in the car. Creative medicine.

Our lungs were clear, but Rich was still so short of breath. We returned home and called the IV nurse again. She came and checked Rich's pulse oxygen level and it read 77%. There was no IV given, instead, we called 911 and Rich was admitted to the hospital while I was sent back home alone.

I didn't realize the shadow was now at the edge. I didn't know. Our church refused to accept anything but a positive outcome. Let the prayer and fasting begin!

I continued to become more and more symptomatic. I had a temperature, no taste, no smell, extreme weakness, fatigue, and absolutely no appetite. I got in touch with a naturopathic doctor who prescribed me the right Covid medications and vitamin combination. My Richard was in isolation on a BiPap machine to help with breathing. I found myself assertively trying to find someone, anyone, who would give me information about him.

Things were about to get more complicated.

I was standing in my kitchen taking my vitamins when I had a Gran Mal seizure. In my fall, I broke three bones in my ankle. It was a very bad break. I called 911 again—twice in one week. That's a bad week!

Now I'm also in isolation in the hospital, and I can't take the medicine my doctor prescribed for me. I'm now under their protocol. No questions asked, no appeals allowed. I lost total control over my healthcare and was isolated.

Strangely, once again, no information was made available to me concerning their plan for me. Hours after I arrived in the emergency room, I was seen by a physician's assistant of the orthopedic MD. She said that we needed to do surgery on my ankle that night. But then I never heard from anyone—not anyone.

For days I asked and no one knew when I was going to have my surgery, nor could they answer why I didn't have it that first night. I was moved out of ER to a Covid floor. After a few days, I had to be moved to a rehab facility to wait for my surgery date, whenever that was going to be. Unfortunately, once you arrive at rehab, your mandatory 14 days of isolation start all over again. My hospital days did not count towards my time.

I still didn't realize that the shadow was rolling in...

In the meantime, our church was being His Church. They weren't just standing, they were pushing back against the spirit of death, darkness, and indifference. They had put poster-size Bible verses all around Rich's hospital bed so that others would see and he would be able to be encouraged by the truth. His favorite was on the wall at the end of his bed:

> Trust in the Lord with all your heart and lean not on your own understanding.
>
> — PROVERBS 3:5

They also made little baggies with the communion elements so that every day, through our phones and FaceTime, Rich and I were able to have communion together. We usually did it with tears. The sense that we were sharing in suffering, the indifference of others, and isolation as our Jesus had, made this time together very personal and precious to us.

Our church community also came to the hospital parking lot at night and prayed for us as well as all the people who were also sick at that time. For seven days they fasted and walked around the hospital praying for the whole medical system in America.

I wish I could say that it was easy in my little isolation room. It was anything but that. I had my Bible. I slept with it. Time with Him was 24 hours. He spoke to me through everything. I guess you could say He was "painfully close"—close through pain.

My church friends are my heroes! They are a living example of the power of God released when God's Church does church.

FOUR

My Walk at Home Begins

I was discharged home two days after my 14-day isolation was over. That made my hospital-rehab stent a total of 21 days. I came home with a cast and wheelchair, needing Depends, and unable to dress or make my meals. I was too weak to take a shower or dry my hair. I had lost 30 pounds. I looked awful. I felt awful. But Jesus loved me. That's all that mattered.

I was confident that with my Jesus we would "make it" but I didn't know what that would look like.

Rich could have only one visitor. I was determined that even though I was weak, unable to drive, and needed a wheelchair, I was somehow going to be that one visitor. I was going to see him! All my wonderful friends were as determined as I was to make that happen.

Being able to touch him was a sweetness like never before. I looked at him and saw our "us." Whenever I felt the swell of tears about the 40 pounds he had lost or the fact that he was too winded to eat, drink, or talk, I looked up at those Bible verses. They were our reality. Not our skinny, saggy broken bodies.

But I admit, sometimes I just wept and wept and wept. I missed him so very much. I couldn't even stand and give him a hug and a kiss because of my leg! If ever I needed to be strong, it would be now! But I wasn't. I just wasn't.

What would I do? To be honest, I positioned my wheelchair as close to Richard as possible and tightly held his hand. I would cry out the only prayer my spirit had the strength to pray, "Help me, Jesus! Help me, Jesus! Help me, Jesus! Help me, Jesus!" Then I'd blow my nose, cry some more, and pray out, "Help me, Jesus! Help me, Jesus! Help me, Jesus!" Repeat, repeat, and repeat. How long? As long as it takes for peace to come.

Sometimes during times like this, He'll give me direction on what to do to get to that peace.

 Cast your cares upon him, for he cares for you.

— 1 PETER 5:7

Jesus and I have a long prayer because of my short "Help me, Jesus!" prayer. I end with amazement. He cares about my cares.

There was a time in my spiritual youth when I pictured myself as a warrior with my hand on God's shoulder saying, "Okay, where's the next battle?" Although that's definitely part of my spiritual person, I also have another picture.

I'm also an intensely loved child snuggled tightly right on Daddy's lap. That's the spiritual person I am right now. With tears and Kleenex, I just can't do much "casting." I do "rolling" over to Him. I do "handing" over to Him. I'm on His lap after all. It's not very far. So, I ask Him to give my Richard the closeness and intimacy I can't. I ask Him to give him the breath that only He can. I ask that He take the pain away. I ask that He tell Rich that it's okay for him to wear cowboy boots! I won't tease him! I ask Him to tell him something funny because "Remember, you made him love to laugh!"

I think I'll be on His lap for a while. But I'll be "warrior ready" soon... well, eventually. God hasn't put a time limit on His lap time. He won't allow me to put that limit on myself either.

FIVE
The Shadow Has Arrived

Through my many years of knowing Jesus and bringing Him into my crises, I've learned to stop and look for Him. His very proactive hand has always been there.

In the beginning, we did that too. We stopped. We looked. We saw. He was always already there.

A couple of months before we got sick, Rich and I both sensed that something very large was going to happen. Although we didn't know the specifics, we did some fasting and prayer in preparation. Little did we know, God was preparing us for what was coming.

I remember a couple of weeks before, while walking through our home office, I said to Rich, "Honey, you need to show me how you do the finances because if you died or something, I wouldn't have a clue what to do!"

About one month before that, Rich felt we needed to sell one car and be a one-car family.

Another amazing thing happened at his job. Although he was retired, he drove a school bus for the local school district. For the first time in the district's history, they were offering the drivers an extra $60,000 in life insurance. That was so wonderful since Rich only had $13,000! Our Jesus—we didn't know, but He did!

It was so encouraging, especially in the shadow, to know that God was there *before* the shadow. It endeared our hearts to Him once again to see that He is involved and not distant and indifferent.

On Oct 12, 2021, after 42 days in the hospital, my Richard breathed his last breath. There are other ways to say it. He died. He passed on. He crossed over. But my heart's cry wanted to say it like this, "Richard left. He left me behind. He left me alone." I've lost my love and best friend, my biggest fan, my knight in shining armor. I've lost half of my one. How do I do one?

It was surreal being rolled out of the hospital in my wheelchair leaving him behind! I hadn't been "Richard-less" for 50 years! How could this be me? The "Covid fog" amplified my inability to take control of myself or even begin to discuss the details of the realities of death; what to do with the body, do you want cremation? How do I pay for everything? People need to be notified. The Celebration of Life details. I was overwhelmed. That word was just not big enough. Things need to be done. Becky was undone. Becky was emotionally unavailable.

I can only describe my sorrow and sadness that first day by likening it to David and his mighty men in 1 Samuel 30. They too had lost their family. If you don't know the story, he and his men came home to Ziklag and found that their enemy, the Amalekites, had burned their town and taken all of their wives and children captive.

 Then David and the people that were with him lifted up their voice and wept, until they had no power to weep anymore.

— 1 SAMUEL 30:4

That was me.

There was such a deep sense of loss that left me with a feeling of hollowness that I'd never heard of or felt before. Fear grabbed my heart and squeezed out all but a drop of hope. But my faith told me that when your hope is in Jesus, a drop is all you need.

While I wept and prayed, wept and prayed, wept and prayed, I missed Rich. Contributing to all of the needed arrangements was an impossibility for me. I couldn't do it emotionally, physically, or spiritually. But God gave me His covering. It was like a big love blanket.

My wonderful family and church covered every detail and more! They all had grace for that. Helping Jesus to love on His Becky was a delight to them. That's how they all made me feel. More tears. These are of a different kind. These are love and gratefulness tears. I've never cried so many.

It's been some four months now. I still have boxes of Kleenex scattered throughout my house. I never know when I might have a "Richard moment." Looking back, I see I've used my old "walk principle" to survive. That's a term I use to describe how I keep going when I want to just give up.

...but David encouraged himself in the Lord his God.

— 1 SAMUEL 30:6

I call it "feeding my heart the truth." I motivate myself to do *God* during hard times. This has been beyond hard. I spend time in the Word, I "talk God, breath God, shout God." I do it by myself. It's personal to me and God.

In my worse-than-overwhelming time, I sensed there was something God wanted to show *us*. All of a sudden, my prayers changed from praying singularly for myself to plural for all of us. Not just *the* Bride, Becky, but the Bride of Christ—the Church. He was revealing that His heart for the Church is the same as His heart for me.

I had prayed about the disconnection of the "Bride of Christ" to the real heart of Jesus, our Bridegroom, for years. I sensed it was on *His* heart as He prepared His Bride for His coming. Now I could *see* how He saw the Church's heart and what it needed... a deeper, intimate revelation of the love of the Bridegroom, Jesus. He knew my heart. He heard every single prayer I have ever prayed. This was something I'd asked Him for in intercession—to see us as He sees us and to know His heart for His people.

A question I pondered was, "Why now? Why reveal this to me now amid so much darkness and turmoil?"

I wanted to say, "Don't pester me with praying for the *whole* Church now! I've got too much! I just can't do anymore! I just want to be Becky your Bride," and grab my Kleenex, blow my nose, and cry. But that little "God nudge" was still there. It never left.

He kept whispering, "Bride." I didn't understand. I wasn't going to pray for the Church when I was just trying to survive! But now I get it. He wasn't asking me to intercede. He was giving me my name: Bride. The Father was involved in this too!

SIX
Then The Light Came

One day shortly after Rich died, I was sobbing. It was more like a loud wailing. Suddenly, I heard Jesus whisper my name, *"Becky."*

The power of His whisper always amazes me. I can hear it no matter what the circumstances are. One word, my name, and all sobbing stopped. The silence was thick, wrapped in anticipation. I expected the calm, optimistic, peaceful voice I'd grown to love so much. It was that and more. *"I want to be your husband."*

What? I almost wanted Him to repeat it. The voice was different. It was dripping with honor. It was so personal and intimate. I guess I never thought He honored me. I never even imagined it. It startled me. But my spirit was prepared. It's like it jumped up with a deep, deep, "YES!"

I realized at that moment that my Richard also had a heart of honor toward me. Jesus' question came with that intimate husband tone with which I was so familiar. It made me feel closer to Jesus than ever before. Rich was home. Jesus was home. Tears came and Kleenexes were used. I've known Jesus as a brother and friend, Savior and King but this was different. I was going home again. Jesus was my Bridegroom. My kingly husband. I was His Bride.

But how could my spirit be so ready? That was a puzzlement to me. Of course, I knew the words "Bride of Christ." I had read them in the Bible and prayed for the Bride of Christ all of my 45 years of knowing Jesus, but I never really thought of what that meant personally. I was praying for the whole Church in a huge "arranged marriage" kind of way!

But then I "got it"! I even understood why the Father was whispering "Bride" to me. I was not only praying for the Church but I was also praying for me! He wanted to be my Bridegroom. My prayers all those years had prepared *my* spirit. It was so ready to say yes. It was time!

This intimate interaction with Jesus changed my mourning and my life. I was basking in the thrill of it when The Holy Spirit unexpectedly interrupted. (What a wonderful family this is!) It seemed almost inappropriate, yet it felt right. He does that, shows the bigness of God, and surprisingly everything fits!

You see, my Jesus can be doing and preparing us for His bigness (praying for the whole Body of Christ) and intimacy (preparing me for this moment, His proposal day) at the same time. All these years, that's what He was lovingly doing for me as I prayed for the "Bride of Christ." Only He is powerful enough to do BIG and INTIMATE at the same time! Oh, the awe of Him! My Bridegroom.

This was an answer to my prayer! That "we've got to get ready" prayer I'd prayed and fasted for the Church—now I was given those revelations I had prayed for, to see how our hearts get prepared for Him and His intimacy when we pray for more of Him. He was asking me, inviting me, to join Him into His intimacy and His bigness. To know and live life with Him that way. To live in a new house... a big house. Now I'm thrilled *and* excited!

I was being invited to have His reality be my new reality. I can tell others what our Bridegroom is like, of His big and intimate heart for us. I can show others. Even in the shadow, I knew this was something I was going to wholeheartedly embrace. But how? That's yet another exciting part of this journey.

SEVEN

A Different Covid Walk

The practical chaos of my life was still my reality but there was a definite change with my new understanding. I wish I could say that the fatigue and sadness disappeared and that I spent my days dancing for my Bridegroom, Jesus. It didn't and I didn't. But there was something new.

For the first time in weeks, I felt a "Go this way" sign in my heart again. I had some understanding and vision again. It was just a little sign often blurred by tears, but it gave me some direction. It was something I could actually "go for" when I felt so very empty. The sense of loss was leaking out and being exchanged with vision.

The shadow was lifting. Surprisingly, that brought a new challenge. Every morning I knew I had a choice. Problem or promise? What was I going to center my thoughts on today? Was it going to be the many problems I had as a result of Rich's death or was it the promise I made to learn how to be the Bride of Jesus? One was a "shadow chaser" and one was a "shadow embracer."

Most days I chose to be a "chaser." But there were days when I chose "embracer." Those are the days I'm totally overwhelmed, and I just want to point my finger at all my problems and whine. Jesus understands. No bolt of lightning comes down and zaps my pointy finger. He waits to be invited into the solution. Now I've switched from problem to promise.

It took me a while to realize this is all Bride training. Just how many times did Richard wait for me while I ranted on about something? Yes, on-the-job Bride training. It felt almost like when Rich was trying to teach me, a very non-computer person, how to use the computer. "If you'd just learn how the computer thinks it'd be so much easier!" Unfortunately, I wasn't interested in learning, and it never got much easier. However, I have a whole different enthusiasm for my Bridegroom, Jesus, and His Bride training.

The Father even gets credit for that! I remember years ago, someone telling me,

"It takes God to love God." So it does! The Father had truly embraced this new bride with a new grace, giving me the motivation to learn how my Bridegroom thinks, during a time when chaotic thoughts were yelling the loudest.

EIGHT
Put On Your Covid Clothes!

PUTTING ON OUR BRIDAL GOWN AND BRIDAL SHOES

Saying, "I'm the Bride of Jesus" and *being* the Bride of Jesus are two different things. *Being* the Bride of Jesus is totally by faith. Faith is the conviction of things NOT SEEN.

The "Becky picture" was not looking good. No sane person would have thought, *Oh, I would really like to marry Becky!*

Bride material I was not. I had never in my entire 45 years of faith been so spiritually weak, with only one drop of hope. I've always taught others the importance of praise. Now I just offered the sacrifice of praise. Physically, I looked like someone coming from a prison camp, having lost 30 pounds. I lost my love, my God-buddy, and my best friend so I was unsure of how I was even going to do life! I looked like a mess!

NINE
Faith Place, A "His Truth" Place, My New Residence

His revelation changes everything! It was so simple that even with Kleenex in hand, my spirit leaped with the truth of it. It was as if it had been waiting for it.

I was asked by Jesus to be His Bride. Yes, that was the truth. I was His choice. That was also the truth. He found me impressive. Once again, truth. He loved me. That's the truth.

My Jesus lives in that "Faith Place." He always lived in the truth of His Bridegroom's love for me. That included all that He did for me because of that love. That included the Cross. He truly sees me as complete and perfect. That's His truth. That's where He lives. He stays there. He invited me to move into that place too. For me, it's still in the "faith" zone. I believe in the power of the Cross, by faith, because of *that* day. I take communion daily now, because of *that* day so I don't forget to say, "You really are *my* Bridegroom!" with joy and complete amazement in my heart!

I changed my clothes.

So I took off my spiritual hospital slippers and put on my Bridal shoes. I took off my spiritual hospital gown and put on my spiritual bridal gown. It didn't feel right at first. The words to describe my look would be ridiculous, unimpressive, and expired. But to Him, my spirit was beautiful, perfect, and inspired.

My first thought was that the enemy must be laughing. But now I realize that he was not. He was groaning. The spiritual hospital gown and slippers were his bridal clothes. He lost because now I can embrace my future destiny, walk in my Bride authority, and walk right out of his shadow. Yes, he's groaning but all of Heaven is loving the gown!

I started to declare who I was and who my Bridegroom was. Though I was unsure of what that meant in my life, it was a truth, and I tried to make every word I spoke based on faith, the conviction of things not seen.

The truth of our life is in God's Word. He makes it simple. We're made in His image and so my declaration makes a difference. It creates things. That's how the faith place works. That's "working from home"—only it's His home!

 ...Let the weak say I am strong.

— JOEL 3:10

I declare, "Becky is the Bride of Jesus. He asked and I said yes. I walk in His strength and authority. Therefore, even when I'm weak, I am strong!"

TEN

Walking Out From Shadow to the Son

Describing my Richard would be easy. He was a man of honor. He was so talented! He was mechanical, so he was good with broken things. He worked in construction, so he could build things for me. He was an electrician, so he could do most anything electrical: put in sockets, fix lights, or put in patio lights. He was good with cars, so he did minor repairs, kept them clean, and monitored oil, tires, and battery. He was good with the yard and the pool, so they got the proper maintenance. He had his own business, so he did all the finances on the computer. The list goes on and on.

But all that Richard was, I very often was not. I had different strengths. That made us a good team. But we had to learn to work together. After 50 years we were good at it.

Embracing A New Normal

These past three months, my Bridegroom, Jesus, has shared with me who He is. Just like with Richard, by learning who He is, I'm able to see how we are going to do Bride and Groom together. It's so simple that it may not seem important enough to write about, but it is. It's all about who He is.

My Bridegroom Loves to Love Me

Now I see it! There are no needs in heaven because Jesus needs nothing. Jesus is completely complete without me. He does not need me as if He wouldn't be whole without me. He wants me because He wants to love me!

 Most assuredly, I say to you, whatever you ask in my name, He will give it to you.

— JOHN 16:23

What? Jesus, my Bridegroom, is so excited about me that He is telling me to ask for whatever I want! "Just tell Dad I told you to ask and you'll always get it." He loves loving His wife, most assuredly!

So one would think that such a wonderful revelation as that would stick to your heart. I have days when I have my wedding dress all pressed and proper. Then there are others where it has spots and wrinkles.

Understanding and living the magnitude of His Bridal love is a process for me. I grew up in a dysfunctional home. My stepfather was verbally and physically abusive. I do not remember him ever hugging me or saying, "I love you." To ask for anything greater than a "need" was unheard of.

Rich, in his gentleness and generosity, was my step toward having Jesus as my Bridegroom. I see that now. The bigness and grandness of Jesus *wanting* to love me as His wife and *wanting* me to ask for my wants would have been an impossibility in my brokenness without my wonderful Richard's beginnings.

But now it's Bridal training. It's that process.

 Therefore, a man should **leave** his father and his mother and should **cleave** to his wife, and the two of them shall be one flesh.

— EPHESIANS 5:31

Although this verse is not specifically talking about me as a Bride of Jesus, there is a principle here that Jesus revealed that would help me in my transition. First, I need to **leave** the old way of thinking. Then I need to **cleave** (biblical meaning is to be glued together) to the new revelations that my new Bridegroom, Jesus, is giving me about being His Bride.

> ...and to be renewed in the spirit of your minds...
>
> — EPHESIANS 4:23

I am working on getting totally out of the shadow and standing tall in the SON.

My Husband is Kind

> But when **the kindness** and love of God our Savior appeared, he saved us.
>
> — TITUS 3:4

I've never really thought much about the kindness of Jesus. I lumped it into His love. But I am here to say, it's different.

I now see His kindness as a part of who He is, His makeup and personality. That means that He will always be kind to me because that is who He is. He never changes. That means it doesn't matter if I'm sobbing and in spiritual numbness, He's there, so kindness is there and always available to me.

The Holy Spirit was giving me eyes to see Him differently. In my crisis, His kind personality was shown through an abundance of people. I have never experienced such caring and generosity! But if my Bridegroom, Jesus, was there, His kindness was too.

Total strangers dropped off groceries, pizza was delivered anonymously, money came in for my bills, my car got washed, and my yard was kept beautiful by total strangers! That list goes on and on. The details are astounding!

In Bride training, I learned that my Bridegroom, Jesus, cannot be anything other than who He is. He is powerful. He is kind. I now realize that His kindness is a weapon. It pushes back the shadow. When it was used *for* me, it dissolved my sorrow and replaced it with peace. That was an unexpected and unearned response in my heart.

I'm going to remember that power and spread kindness. I need to "show off" my Bridegroom and let His kindness shine and peace abound.

My Bridegroom is Patient

Jesus, my Bridegroom, lives in that "spiritual space." He's not like Rich sitting on the couch watching TV with me or helping me make dinner. That seems obvious, right? But when He asked me to be His Bride, I was invited into that spiritual space in a very real and practical way.

I am progressing, I'm happy to report! There's a whole different kind of intimacy available for His Bride. That empty couch doesn't seem as empty as it did. I don't feel the desperate loneliness that I did. In a very unreligious way, but a very real way, He's on the couch with me. The more I get to know Him in this more intimate way, that desire for "husband closeness" is being filled with "Bridegroom closeness" that is ever-present in my ever-ready spirit.

I like His Bride training!

Sometimes with Kleenex in hand, I'm choosing the promise and not the problem. I'm set on being a "spiritual" bride to my "spiritual" Bridegroom! No matter how long it takes. Jesus is agreeable to that. He not only loves me but He loves me in my process!

My heart's cry is for "sharper eyes to see and ears to hear." Admittedly, sometimes the request is a frustrated one, laced with urgency. Although not as often. But I know that I'll function much better in my new spiritual "home" with sharp spiritual eyes and ears.

ELEVEN
My Exhortation to Us, His Bride, The Church

Our Bridegroom is wanting to encourage, reset, and realign us. By the Cross, the wedding has been paid for. Through the difficulty and pain of our life and our times, we must step up and walk into that lofty position and relationship.

The hour that we are called to is an hour that will require power and a revelational relationship. We can and must understand and be able to walk in His "Bridegroom" authority. He's given that authority to us, His Bride, to spiritually invade and change our world.

This is not a time to demand *safety*. Do not embrace a "wait and see" relationship with Him for you will not see Him because you will not have the spiritual eyes to see.

Matthew 26:41 tells us to **"Watch and pray**." Don't just look. Watch. Keep your eyes on what is happening in the world and the Church. As His Bride, you need to be aware of what your Bridegroom is doing and what His plan is. You have His heart, and He has yours. You are a part of His plan because you're a part of Him.

Pray. All the time. He longs to have His access to you be a supernaturally normal thing. Stay involved and connected in that intimate Bridal relationship. Share and discuss the things that make His heart beat. (That includes you, by the way.) As your heart becomes one with His, you'll start to see how He enjoys the nations and loves those whom the rest of the world sees as unlovable.

This is not a time for indecision or delay. Decide. Commit. Cry out to Him, "Oh, Bridegroom, Jesus! I'm in awe of you! Revive me! Renew me! I desperately want to be your Bride! I put on my wedding dress and bridal shoes!"

What happens then?

Your life will change.

TWELVE
My Conclusion, My Reality

The impossible has happened to me. The most horrific time in my life has turned into a new life. I'm no longer a widow. I have a Bridegroom. His name is Jesus. I'm His Bride.

I will always be in Bridal training. My sense of loss has left because of what I've found. I love people more. Some say that suffering will do that. No, I know Him differently, I have His heart, His love, how can I not love more? I laugh more and my smile is bigger. Of course, I would! I'm married to Jesus! He has no impossibilities, is always optimistic, and He loves to laugh! He did invent giggles, after all. I trust more. In the shadow He valued me. He rescued me. It would go against who He is to do anything else to His Bride. I truly know that now.

I'm now a singer of two very simple little songs. One's for enjoying the new love for me as He takes a love glance my way:

> *I will walk and I will see*
> *I will walk and I will see*
> *I will walk and I will see*
> *You look at me*

One's for the times I need reminding of who I am:

You're not a widow, you're a Bride you see
It's you, Becky, now you're with Me.

I'm Out Of The Shadow

> O death, where is your victory? O death, where is your sting?
>
> — 1 CORINTHIANS 15:55

> He will wipe away every tear from their eyes, and death shall be no more, neither shall there be mourning, no crying, no pain anymore, whether former things have passed away.
>
> — REVELATION 21:4

> ...and we know that in all things God works for the good of those who love him who have been called according to his purpose.
>
> — ROMANS 8:28

Walking It Out

I'm ending with a simple little story with a supernatural beginning. About 10 years ago (maybe longer, Richard was the date guy!), I came in my front door and God said, "Sit down. We're going to write a book." I grabbed my iPad and began to peck away as He dictated this story to me. Herbie was born.

I'm sharing it now because it's a perfect story of our Christian journey. It has many spiritual lessons and parallels in it but the ending is fabulous because Herbie goes from Bridesmaid to Bride. Herbie is changed. He's elevated. He's no longer crawling on the earth. He's flying. His heart is now beating in sync with the heart of God.

Under our wedding gown beats a "Herbie heart," flying in the Spirit as the Bride of Jesus. Could there ever be a greater privilege? I think not.

THIRTEEN

Herbie

Once upon a time, there was a little green caterpillar named Herbie. He lived in a large forest with huge grand looking trees. How he loved the trees! Somehow, he always felt protected because they were there. *Not even a big bird can see me!*

The small bright-colored flowers always brightened his day, and the delicious greens made his tastebuds tingle.

The floor of the forest was his domain. Each day was an adventure!

Life was good—*mostly*. There was a problem that no one knew about, except Herbie, of course. He didn't tell his friends or even talk about it with his Father God. He tucked it into the pocket of his heart.

The problem was simple. Herbie just didn't feel special. Plain, ordinary, and unimportant are words that he used to describe himself in his self-talk.

"You know you're nothing special, Herbie! All you do is wiggle and chew, wiggle and chew, that's all you do!" Yup, he was certain. He was just a small insignificant little caterpillar. He wasn't important at all.

The truth is that his heart ached every time he thought about it. He carried a little pocket of sadness that no one knew about... or so he thought.

There were also times when Herbie could smile, and widely! He had gotten to know his Father God. The Father made everything different. He made Herbie's heart sing! He always felt more than special during their times together. Herbie lived with a heart of excitement about the Father. He made him feel "big" somehow! But when Herbie was alone, his heart pocket of sadness came right back. Herbie went right back to feeling like nothing special again.

Herbie's life changed when he met Father God. In his excitement, he used every opportunity to tell anyone about Him. One of the most amazing parts was, "He actually talks to me!" It seemed so simple to Herbie. When he told everyone, he expected them to understand. Some did. Some didn't. Herbie never understood why some didn't want to know his wonderful Father God.

One day, as Herbie was enjoying his morning breakfast greens, he heard the Father's wonderful voice. "Herbie, I'd like to spend some special time with you. Would you like that?"

The reply was quick, "Of course! Can't wait!"

Father God invited Herbie to go to a special hiding place in a specific tree. "Right at that spot," He said. "It'll be a hiding place where we won't be noticed. This will be our time, you and Me."

Herbie was excited! He wasn't new to the Father's adventures, so he was quick to start the crawl toward the Father's chosen tree. When he reached the base of the tree, he was exhausted. He looked up, way up!

"Wow, that's a real, real tall tree," he said with a sigh. His thoughts raced. *Do I really want to do this? It's so far up! I'm so tired! Maybe I didn't think this through.* He quickly shook his head to clear his thoughts.

He found himself yelling, "Yes! Herbie, yes! Of course, you're going up! It's the Father! Get going! Get going!" It worked like the sound of a crow flying overhead. Time to focus. The Father was always the priority!

"What are you thinking? Get it together!" he ordered himself. With a clear mind and determination restored, Herbie began his long trek up the tree. He stopped now and then to look down to see how far he'd already gone. Each time his confidence increased, even though it was taking more and more effort.

His determination slowed any recognition of the changes that were happening, but Herbie eventually noticed. His body was doing something strange. "Hmm, I feel weird but I've got to keep going! I've got a long way to go yet!" So he just shrugged his little caterpillar shoulders and refocused on the task at hand. Get to the Father's spot!

By the time he arrived, he felt a great sense of accomplishment! He was physically pooped but his spirit was soaring! *I made it! I'm actually here!* he thought as he patted those caterpillar shoulders in a caterpillar way. But his excitement was distracted when he noticed his two little spots. They were not special spots. All caterpillars have them. They were just there! Just taking up space, I guess you'd say.

But not now! *Wow! I wish the guys could see this! My spots! They're spitting out stuff! They've never done that before! At least, I don't think so. I would've noticed, wouldn't I?* Then he considered that he just got up and went wherever and whenever he wanted to go and just kind of dragged his body along. He didn't pay attention. He shrugged those caterpillar shoulders another time. "Oh, well," he said out loud.

He was more interested in his here and now. He felt the stuff coming out of his spots. It felt almost silky and looked like a thin strand of string. It just kept coming and coming! Herbie's mind was full of thoughts, thoughts he'd never thought before: *This is so weird. Is this stuff ever gonna stop? But it feels right somehow. I don't get it, but my body seems to know what it's doing!"* His body had turned into an exciting mystery!

It wasn't long before he was totally encased in this silky cocoon and stuck to the underside of a leaf. Herbie didn't realize it but the Father had replaced the fear he would have normally had with excitement. "Wow! I didn't know I could even do this!" Herbie yelled.

He knew that there wasn't anyone around to hear him but he felt so snug and warm he just had to say it anyway. Somehow, this all felt right. It felt good! He knew in his "knower" this was all a part of the Father's plan. Once again, the Father had surprised him. Herbie started looking around and checking things out. "You know, Father, it's sure dark in here. You're still with me, aren't you? You're always are." Now, the Father knew very well that Herbie never liked the darkness. But somehow Herbie knew he'd be okay as long as the Father was there.

"Of course," said the Father, "this is like playing hide-and-seek together! No one's going to see us in here!"

"Yeah, but I can't even tell if it's morning or night! You know that, right?"

"We can just stay snuggled and see what happens," the Father replied. "I have a special treat for you. You'll be really surprised!"

Herbie's eyes grew very big with anticipation. Didn't the Father understand?

"Yeah, but I'll have to get out of here before you can give it to me, you know. I can't even wiggle in here!" Instantly Herbie felt the Father's smile, even though he couldn't see him. "I'm glad I've got my inside eyes!" Herbie was so in tune with the Father, that he didn't notice his body changing—changing in ways that would change his life forever.

Herbie had a wonderful time in his little dark cozy cocoon. It made him feel like he was in a never-ending hug from the Father. They talked and talked about all kinds of things. He answered every question Herbie asked. For the first time, Herbie felt content. He felt important and he was loving it. After all, he had the Father all to himself!

One day, the Father told Herbie that it was time to do something new. He asked Herbie to wiggle real, real hard. He was told he would feel something new and different along the side of his body and the Father wanted him to push them out as hard and fast as he could.

Herbie furrowed his brow. "Yeah, but..." Herbie replied, "I think it would be great if we could just keep hangin' out together. I don't understand why I need to do all this hard stuff! Wiggling hard, really hard?"

"You'll understand," said the Father. "I promise, you will love My surprise!"

Once again, Herbie's inside eyes saw His wonderful smile. He felt empowered again and started to wiggle and push like he had never done before in his whole life.

After a while, Herbie was getting tired. "How much longer, Father? I'm pooped!"

"Good job, Herbie, you're almost there!" The Father was quick to answer. Herbie knew he'd answer right away because he could feel He the Father right beside him even though the cocoon was so small. And then, of course, there was his wonderful, peaceful, reassuring smile that gave him the strength to keep going.

"Yeah, but..." Herbie yelled out, "It would be nice to know why I have to do all this hard work!"

"I know, so you'll know when it's time," was all He said. That was somehow enough to make everything okay. Back to wiggles and pushes!

It wasn't long after the Father said those words that Herbie saw the first rays of light break through the darkness of his snug little safe place. He paused in his efforts for a moment to let his eyes adjust to the sunlight. He frowned and thought, *Was it always this bright?* He wasn't sure if he liked the change. For a moment he wondered if he could repair the sides of his cocoon and go back to the dark place he had become so comfortable.

But once again the Father, knowing Herbie better than Herbie knew himself, said, "Keep going, Herbie! You will love it! It will be an adventure we will go through together!" Then, of course, Herbie saw that wonderful smile. But it was different this time. It was not only peaceful and loving but it looked full of excitement and anticipation!

The Father is excited! thought Herbie. *This is going to be great!* He restarted his wiggling and pushing efforts with renewed vigor. "I will break through! I will break through! The Father says it's good so I will break through! I will break through! The Father says it's good so I will break through!" he declared louder and louder, over and over, yelling at the doubts in his heart as well as the walls of his cocoon that he now knew were keeping him from his new adventure with the Father.

It wasn't until Herbie was so tired that he felt he could only muster the strength for only one last push that the walls of the cocoon finally fell away. Immediately, he felt the warmth of the sun. *Umm,* Herbie thought. *This warm is not stuffy like it was in the cocoon! The Father was right! I do like this better!* Herbie quickly looked for a leaf to eat since he was very very hungry! *I didn't feel hungry before but boy, I'm sure hungry now!* Herbie thought. *But somehow, it's different. I don't feel like eating the same way. Huh? How can that be?*

He looked to the left from his tree branch, expecting to find the usual lunch selection. But something blocked his sight! "What is that?" he said with a gasp. Well, it was very unusual, that was for sure! "NO! It's attached to ME!" Herbie was horrified! His heart beat faster. His jaw dropped when he found a matching one on his right side as well!

Herbie had to admit though, that they were very beautiful. Big and bright. Colors and design. Herbie's eyebrows raised with wonder. "I wonder where they came from! What are they are for?" Then the wonder was replaced with a frown. "Oh my, how am I ever going to wiggle with these attached to me?" Herbie shook the left one. It would not come off! Herbie shook the right one. That one wouldn't come off either! Herbie began to worry. *What was the Father thinking?* It was an obvious question he looked forward to asking. Although they were very beautiful, they obviously wouldn't work for him and he didn't know how to get rid of them! The Father would just have to understand and help him!

The Father interrupted his thoughts. "I gave them to you, Herbie. They are My gift to you."

"Yeah, but... Herbie was quick to reply, "don't You realize, I can't wiggle with these! If I can't wiggle I can't get around. If I can't get around I can't live. Didn't You think about that when You were picking out my gift? Now I can't get them off!"

The Father answered in an excited voice, "My dear one, you don't understand the gift that I've given you. But you will. Those new things attached to you are called wings. Not everyone has them. With wings, you can fly.

Herbie thought that the Father was kidding and said, "Yeah, real funny! That's a good one!" Out blurted a loud "Ha! Ha! Ha!" caterpillar belly laugh.

"No, Herbie," grinned the Father, "You can *fly*."

"Yeah, but... " stammered Herbie, "Now really, Father, I thought You would know this since You *made* me and everything, but some things fly and some things don't. I'm on the DON'T fly side."

The Father knowingly shared, "Herbie, while we were having our wonderful snuggle time in the cocoon, you were getting to know Me better, right?"

"Right!" Herbie quickly answered. "It was great, but I had no idea all this was happening!"

"Well," replied the Father, "I was giving you My gift. To do that, I changed you both on the inside and the outside.

Herbie listened closely, trying to understand. The Father continued, "It's not that I thought that you needed to be improved. I loved you as a caterpillar! But Herbie, I made you to *fly*. I want you to have the excitement of flying. You will love it! I've made you for it! Now you're ready for it. Go, My dear, Herbie, FLY, My butterfly!"

Fly? Really? Me? Herbie's thoughts flew through his mind. A wide smile slowly broke across Herbie's face as he blurted, "This is too good to be true! Do you mean, Father, that if I step off this limb I won't tumble to the ground like a blob of goo?"

"That's right!" the Father quickly reassured. "You've got it! You understand! You will not fall. You will rise up in ways like never before in your whole life! You will go places and do things you never dreamed of doing. You will look at things in a way that you have never looked at them before! Believe me, Herbie. Step off the branch and flap your wings. I'll do the rest. Let's have this adventure together!"

Herbie slowly edged to the end of the branch. He was still arguing with himself as he took that first step off. It was the biggest step that Herbie had ever taken. After all, how silly he'd look to the other caterpillars if he fell to the ground and then told them he'd stepped off the branch because he thought he could fly. He thought as he often thought, *I'm just Herbie, nothing special.*

For a few moments, he wrestled with his emotions. "Should I or shouldn't I?" He came to a final decision.

"No! No! No! I've never had anyone as loving and trustworthy as my Father! The Father is *always* there and He *always* knows what to do! He *never* makes fun of me! He *always* laughs at my funnies!" Herbie spoke to his heart, *I am going to listen to my Father!*

The decision was made. He jumped off the branch. Herbie flapped his wings as the Father had told him but also closed his eyes, just in case. He didn't want to see the ground come closer and closer. He wasn't sure if it'd help, but he closed them anyway.

To his surprise, he didn't fall at all! He soared up and up and up. Herbie was so surprised at how easy it was that the fear left and excitement tumbled out of his mouth as he yelled, "Weeeeeeee! Whoopee! Weeeeeeee! Whoopee!" for hours and hours and hours.

Then there was the Father's smile. Herbie saw it as he flew. "See, Herbie?" the Father said. "I knew you'd love My present!" It was as if they were flying side by side!

The sun was going down when Herbie finally landed on a flower's leaf to rest. The Father and Herbie talked about all of the events of the day. The first words that rolled out of Herbie's mouth were, "Yes, Father! Yes! I don't want to crawl around anymore!" Herbie was thrilled with the new things he had seen and experienced. He was talking so fast that it was sometimes hard for him to get the words out in the right order! It was all too fantastic to even put into words!

The Father hugged Herbie's heart and said, "Herbie, I want you to know that I love you. I have always loved you. I want to tell you again so you won't ever forget: there was never anything that needed to be improved. When you were a caterpillar I loved you as much as I love you now.

"Yeah, but... if you liked me as a caterpillar, why did you make me into a butterfly?" Herbie asked.

"Well, Herbie, I love to be creative and make interesting things. That's just the way I am! I love to create! Everything I make is perfect and fun to learn about. When I made the world, I thought that by having caterpillars change into butterflies, everyone would have fun getting to know the creative part of Me better. I knew everyone would be blessed by it. You see, that's why you were changed into a butterfly. It's not that I don't like the caterpillar. I love them! I made them! But remember, Herbie, I just changed the packaging, I didn't change the Herbie! I still have my Herbie! I would *never* risk losing that! I LOVE our time together. When you call My name, it makes My heart beat faster. There is no voice like My Herbie's voice. There is no giggle like My Herbie's giggle. I even love your 'Yeah, buts.'"

"My 'Yeah, buts?' Don't they make You mad? It sure makes my friends mad! Sometimes I even tell You You're wrong! I don't think I should do that, should I?" said Herbie.

"No, I love them. It's you trying to sort things out. It's all a part of the process of getting things to make sense. 'Yeah, buts' are part of any loving relationship. It made My heart hurt when you said you were 'just a caterpillar who wiggled and chewed, wiggled and chewed.' You thought you weren't valuable to anyone because all you did was 'wiggle and chew.' Always remember, Herbie, your value will never be based on what you do or how you look. It's not about whether you have beautiful wings or you can fly. You hold that special place in My heart because of *who* you are. YOU are My one and only you. You are and always will be valuable to Me. You will always be a 'someone of great importance.'

A big smile of relief spread across Herbie's face. His eyes shined. "That's my Dad!"

"Herbie," said the Father, "would you do something for Me?"

"Anything, ask anything and I'll do it," Herbie quickly replied.

"First, if this is too scary for you, I understand. I will not love you any less if you don't want to do it. I also won't love you more if you do. I already love you 100%! Do you understand?"

"Yup! Got it!" said Herbie, eager to listen. *After all*, he thought, *what could He want me to do that could be so bad? The Father never does bad stuff!*

"I have something that weighs heavy on My heart that you would be perfect to help Me with."

"Ask away!" Herbie said in an *"I am determined to bless my Father"* type of voice.

"I shared with you how much I desperately love you and that there's nothing you could ever do to make Me stop loving you, right?"

"Right," said Herbie with a nod.

"You understand how I love to hear your voice. I love to have you jump up on My lap. I love your giggle. I love all of you. You know that, right?"

"That's right. Absolutely. I know it."

"Herbie," replied the Father, with obvious pain in his voice, "there are others who don't know that I love them. Some voices never call My name. They never talk to Me. I long to hear their voices! I miss them so much that My heart aches! Do you understand, Herbie? I miss them.

Would you go and tell them how much I love you and how much I love them?"

"Wow! Would I?" Herbie exclaimed. "I would love to! Sometimes my heart feels like it's going to burst because I love You so much. If all you're asking is to tell others about *that*, I'm not scared at all! Wait until they hear that You actually miss not hearing from them. Okay, that's it? I can do it. I will gladly make that my goal. I will tell everyone I meet. My Father wants to know them. He wants to love them. How do I know? I know because He loves me! He even loves my 'yeah, buts'! He even loves my giggles. I'll tell them that I know way down in my knower, if the Father can love Herbie then He can certainly love them!"

So Herbie was off with a thrilled heart! Who would have thought it would be so easy? Being important is all about being loved by the most important Father ever!

Well, I guess that means you're important too! Because just like Herbie, the Father loves, loves, loves you, and wants to do things with you! This story is just to remind you just in case you ever forget!

So let's go, Bride. We have some flying to do!

FOURTEEN

One Last Chapter!

I thought that was the end of my book.

But He knew that it wasn't done. I had just set the manuscript aside. It's been about three months now (nine months since my Richard died). He told me it's time to finish this book.

As I reread what I've written, I'm amazed by how quickly He's changed me! He's truly loved me so intimately through this time. I didn't realize how I have been changed in ways I can't even express.

It has been an unbelievable time. I am learning the reality of being His Bride. He has brought me into a much larger family than I thought it was! By large, I mean that they do large things! I mean *large things*! And I am being redefined along the way. Let me explain.

Very early in my Bride journey, He spoke to me about His provision for me. He told me that I would be rich. The new revelation of His generous heart and bridal love for me, complete with my wedding dress, made that seem reachable! The fact that I lost three-quarters of my income after my husband's death seemed almost irrelevant. I didn't ask how He was going to do it. I didn't question it. I was full of the revelational knowledge that He loves me as a husband loves a wife. It was like

He had put a stamp on my heart: "Becky is mine!" I knew I'd have an abundance of everything! It was a done deal. I still know that. I love that stamp!

The *show* started to become apparent one night as I crawled into bed. I was tired. I heard Him whisper, "Becky, don't go to bed yet, we're going to write a book." I grabbed my iPad and my first book, *Jesus, Do You Know How To Whisper?* for children was written. It took about 15 minutes.

For the next two weeks, He downloaded another six books. All of them are children's books. I never thought about being an author much less about being a children's book author. I asked Him, "A children's book? Really? You know I'm not a kid person." (I love my kids and grandkids, for sure! But some people just aren't "into kids" and that's me.)

His reply was simple, as it usually is: "Well, I am!" Then He showed me why. That changed everything!

He stirred me with the revelation of His plan to raise up children to be His "hidden power bombs" in this age. He will use them for signs and wonders all over the world. That meant that these books are equipping books! We're going to raise up a generation!

He's also giving a Word to the Church through these little books.

 Truly, I tell you," he said, "unless you change and become like little children, you will never enter the Kingdom of heaven.

— MATTHEW 18:3

He's calling His Church back to childlike faith. I understood now. We're going to bring transformation and reformation! I get to be a part of that!

But how? Well, of course, He had that covered.

Out of the blue, He started to bring people into my life. None of them knew anything about me or my Bride adventures. Many had expertise and connections in marketing and business strategies, web and logo design, and product development. All these wonderful Christian people generously offered to donate their skills and their time to this adventure. All working on these little kids' books.

That's just one of the *large* family "get-togethers" I'm in the middle of as His Bride. There are others. One is even larger than my books! All are out of my expertise. I'm 72. I'm being redefined. It started the minute He said, "Becky, I want to be your husband." And my spirit yelled, "Yes!"

One Last Thought

This is the age when the Heavenly Father is preparing the Bride for His Son. That was His heart and our purpose from the beginning. That Bridal revelation is available to you, as a child of the Father (not as a generic Body of Christ). As I said before, I say again—ask for it. Seek that intimacy.

> *You will seek me and find me when you search for me with all of your heart.*
>
> — JEREMIAH 29:13

You *will* find it, He promises. I am growing to understand more and more every day; being the Bride of Jesus is what I was made to be. It feels so right. It feels so complete.

As for me, I'm at my wedding dance and I'm enjoying "living large!"

> *You have turned my mourning into dancing for me; you have taken off my sackcloth and clothed me with joy.*
>
> — PSALM 30:11-12

Come join me!

Made in the USA
Middletown, DE
30 October 2022

13751794R00035